ONE YEAR FOR LOVE

52 Questions for Couples
to Spark Meaningful Conversations
and Build a Stronger Relationship

TABLE OF CONTENT

Welcome to Your Year of Connection

It is absolutely wonderful and romantic when two people connect in their own special way. Some couples do seem to be made for each other — and when love begins to grow, it's easy to believe that alone will be enough to carry the relationship forward over time. And in many ways, that's true — love is the foundation. But there's another truth: a lasting connection needs more!

Most couples realize — usually after the initial honeymoon phase begins to settle — that communication beyond loving looks and gentle touches becomes essential. Open, honest, and respectful communication is the key to navigating daily responsibilities together, building routines that work for both of you and staying close while juggling everyday life. A reliable and lasting connection needs words. It requires honesty, curiosity, and mutual understanding. The real, long-term connection doesn't happen by accident. It grows through active effort, open communication, and the willingness to keep learning about each other. If you're holding this book, chances are you already know this. And that's amazing! You are already taking the first step on your journey! This book is your invitation to make time for what matters: each other.

One Year for Love is not about being perfect. It's about being present. It's about creating space—in the middle of work responsibilities, family, and otherwise busy schedules—to ask each other fundamental questions, tell your stories, and discover something new about a person you thought you already knew inside out. And, it's about creating a little ritual of connection — to keep the momentum of your honeymoon phase going or to bring back a spark that may have been waiting quietly for your attention.

Why Weekly Questions Work

We don't always need more time together. We need more *meaningful* time together. This book isn't about fixing what's broken. It's about nurturing what's already beautiful. Asking intentional questions regularly helps you slow down, listen deeply, learn something new — even about someone you know well, and ultimately feel seen, heard, and connected.

It's easy to discuss what's for dinner or what needs doing. But when was the last time you asked your partner what lights them up inside? What comforts them when life feels hard? What makes them feel most loved? Understanding this and regularly incorporating each other's needs into your daily routines will contribute to your relationship thriving for years to come.

One thoughtful question can spark a conversation.
One honest answer can deepen your connection for years.

About the Questions

Throughout your 52-week journey, you might notice that some questions fee familiar — or that you are revisiting topics you've already touched on. That's intentional. Relationships grow in layers. Reflection deepens over time.

When this happens, treat it as an opportunity: Are your answers still the same? Would you add something new now that time has passed? Has life shifted your priorities, dreams, or perspective on each other?

Maybe you'll find that what mattered to you then still holds true today — and recognizing that is a powerful insight. Or perhaps you'll be surprised by how much has changed since you first thought about this topic. Both realizations are part of the journey.

How to use this Book

The idea is simple: choose one question per week and let it become your little ritual of connection. Try different times to start off: Maybe it's during Sunday morning coffee, then a quiet evening walk, or maybe one Monday night after work. Find moments that fits your life.

Whenever possible, go screen-free. Take turns answering first. Give each other space to think and speak without rushing. Stay curious — even if you think you already know the answer. Let yourself be surprised. Use the weekly Reflections pages to capture your thoughts, ideas, memories, or plans. There's no right or wrong way to use them — they're here for you to look back on later.

And if a question doesn't feel right for you at this moment — that's okay too. Feel free to skip it and come back later. Sometimes these conversations take a little courage, especially if they're new to your routine. Trust your timing — but try to stay within the flow of the quarter, so you can pause for your seasonal reflection before moving forward.

Most of all — let this be fun! Be kind to each other. Be patient with the process.

And remember: showing up — even imperfectly — is already an act of love.

This is your year for connection.

This is your One Year for Love.

WHAT DOES A "GREAT RELATIONSHIP" MEAN TO YOU – REALLY?

Reflection:

Every person carries their own picture of what love and partnership look like.

A great relationship might mean lots of laughter and fun for one person. For another, it might mean deep conversations and emotional safety. For someone else, it could be about teamwork, shared goals, or physical closeness.

The important part? Your idea of love might not precisely match your partner's. And that's okay. This question helps you understand what matters most to you — in theory, and your everyday life together.

It's about saying: "This is what I dream of when I think about ‚us' at our best."

Try This:

On a separate piece of paper, each of you writes down three words or phrases that describe your version of a dream relationship. Think about:

- How do I want us to feel together?

- What's most important to me in love?

- What would I love to experience more of in our relationship?

Then, share your answers. Compare your words. Notice what overlaps — that's your shared vision. Notice what's different — that's where curiosity and growth live.

WRITE DOWN YOUR COMBINED FINDINGS ON THE REFLECTIONS PAGE.
IT IS YOUR STARTING POINT FOR THE YEAR AHEAD.

REFLECTIONS

....

....

....

....

....

....

....

....

....

....

....

....

....

....

....

DATE ACCOMPLISHED: .... ♡

WHAT DO YOU REMEMBER MOST ABOUT HOW WE FIRST MET OR STARTED DATING?

Reflection:

Every couple has their beginning — sometimes magical, sometimes messy, sometimes funny. Your version of „how we met" might even be slightly different from your partner's — and that's what makes it fun.

Remembering those early moments helps you reconnect with the spark that brought you together. It reminds you of how you saw each other then—with fresh eyes, curiosity, and excitement.

This exercise isn't about getting all the details right. It's about remembering how it felt.

Try This:

Each of you take a moment to tell your side of the story.

- Where were you?

- What did you notice first about the other person?

- What made you smile? What made you nervous?

You can also pull out an old photo, song, or message from those early days and share how it still affects you today.

WRITE DOWN THE BEST MEMORY OR DETAIL ON YOUR REFLECTIONS PAGE — SOMETHING WORTH REMEMBERING REPEATEDLY.

REFLECTIONS

....

....

....

....

....

....

....

....

....

....

....

....

....

....

DATE ACCOMPLISHED: .... ♡

WHAT'S ONE THING I DO (BIG OR SMALL) THAT MAKES YOU FEEL TRULY LOVED AND SEEN?

Reflection:

Love isn't just about grand gestures. More often, it's about the tiny things that make someone feel noticed and cherished. Your role in this, your unique way of making your partner feel loved, is crucial. Maybe it's when your partner makes you a cup of tea without asking. Perhaps it's a kind word, a certain hug, or how they sit beside you when you've had a hard day.

We all have different triggers that we connect with love — things that speak directly to our hearts.

This exercise aims to understand and appreciate the unique ways your partner expresses their love.

Try This:

You share one or two things your partner does that make you feel deeply loved. It might surprise you. It might be something they don't even realize is so powerful.

WRITE THEM DOWN ON YOUR REFLECTIONS PAGE —
AS LITTLE LOVE INSTRUCTIONS TO RETURN TO ANYTIME.

REFLECTIONS

....

....

....

....

....

....

....

....

....

....

....

....

....

....

DATE ACCOMPLISHED: .... ♡

WHAT HELPS YOU FEEL MOST SUPPORTED WHEN YOU'RE STRESSED OR OVERWHELMED?

Reflection:

Stress brings out different sides in all of us.

Some people need space and quiet.

Others need hugs and words of reassurance.

Some want help solving the problem.

Others want to vent without advice.

This question helps you learn how to show up for your partner during challenging moments — in the way that feels most loving to them.

Try This:

Each of you shares 2-3 things that help you feel cared for when stressed.

Example answers:

- "Please don't try to fix it — just listen."
- "Hugs help me reset."
- "Offer to take something off my plate."

WRITE THEM DOWN ON YOUR REFLECTIONS PAGE —
THIS BECOMES YOUR PERSONALIZED STRESS CARE MANUAL.

REFLECTIONS

....

....

....

....

....

....

....

....

....

....

....

....

....

DATE ACCOMPLISHED: .... ♡

How to Stay On Track
(Especially When Life Gets Busy)

One month in already! That's something to be proud of! It speaks to your dedication, love, and willingness to show up for your relationship—not just in theory but in practice. This dedication and commitment set you apart from many people who want to work on their relationship but never quite start. You didn't just start — you stayed. And that deserves to be celebrated. Treat yourself to something this week!

To help you keep the momentum going, here are some tips for the weeks (and months) ahead. Because here's the truth: Most beautiful ideas in life don't fade because they weren't good enough. They fade because life gets busy. We all start with energy and great intentions: "This will be our new ritual!" And then life happens. Work deadlines pile up, kids get sick, weekends fill up, and fatigue sets in. And we tell ourselves: „It's fine — we'll catch up next week... maybe we'll do two questions at once." And before you know it, a month has passed — and this little book is gathering dust somewhere.

Entering this procrastination spiral is human and happens naturally. Getting out in time to continue working towards your goal successfully needs intention. So, here is your gentle reminder: This book is not about perfection. It's about your relationship. It's about making space for connection, *especially* when life feels full.

So, take a moment to celebrate your dedication with whatever feels like a little reward - your favorite tea, a glass of wine, take-out, or simply a quiet moment together. Enjoy it, and get excited to continue the journey!

HELPFUL TIPS

1

Revisit the time you picked for your conversations. Did it work well for both of you? Or did life often get in the way? Look back and be honest.
Then choose a time that feels realistic and good for this next stretch. Commit to it for the next 8 weeks and treat it like a small promise to your relationship.

2

Set a reminder on your phone — not to nag, but to protect this space. Call it something loving like: "Us Time" or "Love Check-In."

3

Keep the book visible. Leave it on your coffee table, nightstand, or next to your favorite mugs.

4

Don't try to "catch up" with multiple questions simultaneously. Start fresh if you missed a week (or two or five). This isn't homework. It's heart work.

5

Celebrate what you *are* doing — not what you missed. Even ten real conversations this year can make a difference. That said, do your best to make your way through all 52 questions, even if it takes you longer than a year. The pace doesn't matter as much as the commitment to keep coming back.

WHAT BOUNDARY HELPS YOU FEEL RESPECTED OR SAFE IN YOUR RELATIONSHIP?

Reflection:

Boundaries are not about keeping each other out but about creating clarity and care within your relationship.

They help us understand what each person needs to feel comfortable, respected, and at ease as individuals and partners.

Clear boundaries can prevent misunderstandings and help love to feel lighter and more relaxed. Everyone knows what's okay and what's not.

This conversation is a chance to share what matters to you so you can support each other in the best possible way.

Try This:

Each of you shares:

- What boundary makes me feel cared for?

- Is there a boundary I'd like to set or strengthen?

WRITE DOWN YOUR BOUNDARIES ON YOUR REFLECTIONS PAGE — NOT AS RULES, BUT AS LOVE AGREEMENTS.

Examples could be:

- *"I need my morning quiet time."*

- *"Please check with me before inviting people over."*

- *"Let's agree on tech-free meals."*

REFLECTIONS

....

....

....

....

....

....

....

....

....

....

....

....

....

....

....

DATE ACCOMPLISHED: .... ♡

HOW DO YOU MOST LIKE TO GIVE AND RECEIVE LOVE?

Reflection:

We often show love in the way we want to receive it.But sometimes your partner speaks a different "love language" — and what feels meaningful to you might not feel as powerful to them. Knowing your love languages helps avoid missing signals and ensures your efforts land right in their hearts.

Here's a quick overview of the 5 Love Languages:

- *Words of Affirmation* — You feel loved when you hear kind words, compliments, or encouragement. A simple "Thank you" or "I'm proud of you" can mean everything.

- *Quality Time* — You feel loved when someone gives you their full attention — undistracted and present. Time spent talking, doing something together, or going for a walk might feel most valuable.

- *Acts of Service* — You feel loved when someone helps lighten your load. Small thoughtful actions — like making coffee, running an errand, or handling a task — show care.

- *Receiving Gifts* — You feel loved when someone gives you something thoughtful — big or small. It's not about material value, but about the meaning behind the gesture.

- *Physical Touch* — You feel loved through physical closeness — like hugs, holding hands, sitting close, or a gentle touch on the shoulder.

Most people appreciate a little of all of them — but often one or two stand out the most.

Try this:

Take turns sharing what makes you feel most loved and cared for, and what's one thing you could do more to speak your partner's love language?

WRITE DOWN YOUR ANSWERS ON THE REFLECTIONS PAGE AS A GUIDE TO ENRICH YOUR EVERYDAY INTERACTIONS.

REFLECTIONS

....

....

....

....

....

....

....

....

....

....

....

....

....

DATE ACCOMPLISHED: .... ♡

WHAT'S SOMETHING YOU DREAM OF DOING, HAVING, OR EXPERIENCING IN THE NEXT 5 YEARS?

Reflection:

Dreaming together keeps your relationship alive and forward-looking.

It's easy to get caught up in daily routines and forget that you're not just partners in logistics — you're partners in life.

Some dreams might feel big and exciting — like traveling to a new country, starting a family, or moving to your dream home.

Others might be simple but just as important — like learning a new hobby together, creating a garden, or having slow Sunday mornings.

Both kinds of dreams tell a story about what matters most to you.

Try This:

Take turns sharing a dream or wish you have for your life together in the next few years.

Ask:

- What would I like to do, have or experience?

- Why does this dream matter to me?

- How would it feel to make this happen together?

WRITE DOWN YOUR DREAMS ON YOUR REFLECTIONS PAGE — EVEN THE SMALL ONES. THESE ARE SEEDS YOU CAN START NOURISHING TOGETHER NOW!

REFLECTIONS

....

....

....

....

....

....

....

....

....

....

....

....

....

....

DATE ACCOMPLISHED: .... ♡

WHAT'S ONE THING I COULD DO MORE OFTEN TO HELP YOU FEEL TRULY VALUED?

Reflection:

Feeling loved is wonderful, but feeling *valued* adds something deeper. It's about knowing that your efforts, presence, and personality are seen and appreciated, not just expected or assumed.

Sometimes, even a small acknowledgment can shift everything. This week is about understanding how your partner feels most recognized — and making sure they know just how much they matter.

Try This:

Ask each other:

- What helps me feel noticed, respected, or appreciated in daily life?

- Is there something you already do that really means a lot — even if you don't realize it?

- What would make me feel more valued on an ordinary day?

WRITE YOUR ANSWERS ON THE REFLECTIONS PAGE,
AND LOOK FOR WAYS TO PRACTICE THESE SMALL HABITS IN THE WEEK AHEAD.
THEY OFTEN MATTER MORE THAN WE THINK.

Examples Might Include:

- *Saying thank you for everyday things, such as …*

- *Noticing when I've gone the extra mile when I do ….*

- *Asking for my thoughts, input, or advice.*

REFLECTIONS

....

....

....

....

....

....

....

....

....

....

....

....

....

....

DATE ACCOMPLISHED: .... ♡

WHAT HELPS YOU FEEL SAFE DURING A DISAGREEMENT OR TOUGH CONVERSATION?

Reflection:

Every couple disagrees from time to time. That's completely normal. But how you navigate those moments makes all the difference. Learning how to handle difficult conversations with care builds trust, emotional safety, and long-term connection.

Some people feel safest when things stay calm and quiet. Others need time and space to think before responding. Some feel comforted by gentle touch or words of reassurance. Others need clear structure or boundaries to avoid getting overwhelmed.

The goal of this week's question isn't to avoid conflict — it's to understand what helps both of you stay respectful, kind, and connected even when you don't agree.

Try This:

Take turns sharing:

- What helps me feel calm and safe during conflict?
- What tends to escalate or hurt me in those moments?
- How can we both handle future disagreements with more care?

WRITE DOWN 2–3 PERSONAL „GROUND RULES" ON YOUR REFLECTIONS PAGE. THESE ARE SMALL AGREEMENTS THAT HELP YOU BOTH FEEL RESPECTED AND SAFE, EVEN IN DIFFICULT MOMENTS.

Examples of Helpful Ground Rules:

- *Speak in a calm voice — even if emotions are strong.*
- *No interrupting — let each person finish their thoughts.*
- *Take a short break to cool down if things get heated.*
- *Reassure each other: "I'm upset, but I still love you."*
- *Return to the conversation when you're both ready — with kindness.*

REFLECTIONS

....

....

....

....

....

....

....

....

....

....

....

....

....

DATE ACCOMPLISHED: .... ♡

WHAT'S A SMALL RITUAL OR ROUTINE YOU'D LOVE US TO START DOING TOGETHER?

Reflection:

As you probably know by now, rituals are small but mighty. They create consistency, safety, and connection in relationships. They tell your partner: *"No matter how busy or stressful life gets, we have this little moment just for us."*

It might be as simple as a morning coffee together without phones, or a goodnight kiss, no matter what kind of day you've had.

These little rituals are like love anchors — keeping you connected even when life feels busy.

Try This:

Each of you shares:

- What ritual or habit would feel memorable or comforting to me?

- When could we start this — daily, weekly, or whenever it fits naturally?

- What would help us protect this time and keep it going?

CHOOSE ONE IDEA AND WRITE IT ON YOUR REFLECTIONS PAGE — AS A LITTLE PROMISE TO KEEP COMING BACK TO.

Examples:

- *Sunday morning walks — to talk, dream, or simply enjoy nature together.*
- *Sharing three things you're grateful for before bed — to end the day on a positive note.*
- *A weekly „no-screen dinner" — where phones stay away, and conversation stays present.*
- *Cooking or planning a meal together once a week.*

REFLECTIONS

....

....

....

....

....

....

....

....

....

....

....

....

....

....

DATE ACCOMPLISHED: .... ♡

WHAT'S SOMETHING SILLY OR WEIRD THAT ALWAYS MAKES YOU LAUGH OR SMILE?

Reflection:

Laughter is connection. It reminds us not to take life—or ourselves—too seriously, helps us let go of stress, and brings us closer in a way that no deep talk ever could.

But here's the thing — it's not always easy to come up with funny moments on the spot. Most of the time, the things that make us laugh happen in the middle of ordinary life:

- A silly comment in the kitchen.

- A shared look during an awkward moment.

- An inside joke born from a past trip or funny mistake.

That's what makes humor so special — it belongs to you.

Try This:

Take a moment to remember:

- What's a funny story from your time together?

- Is there an inside joke you still use?

- What was a situation that left you both laughing uncontrollably?

If nothing comes to mind right now — no pressure. Instead, create your very own Feel-Good Fun List:Write down your top 3 favorite funny movies, shows, or comedy specials.

This list will be your go-to for a day when life feels heavy, and all you need is a good laugh together.

WRITE YOUR MEMORIES — OR YOUR FUN LIST — ON THE REFLECTIONS PAGE.

REFLECTIONS

....

....

....

....

....

....

....

....

....

....

....

....

....

....

DATE ACCOMPLISHED: .... ♡

WHAT DO I SAY (OR COULD SAY) TO MAKE YOU FEEL LOVED OR CONFIDENT?

Reflection:

Words shape how we see ourselves — and how we feel in our relationship.

Some people light up when they hear: *"I'm proud of you."* Others melt when they hear: *"I'm so lucky to have you."* Or maybe it's something playful — like a nickname only you use.

Kind words have staying power. This week is about learning what words really matter to your partner — so you can use them more often and with intention.

Try This:

Take turns sharing:

- What words or compliments feel especially meaningful to me?

- What would I love to hear more often from you?

- Is there something you'd like to hear that I don't say often enough?

WRITE THESE LITTLE LOVE SCRIPTS ON YOUR REFLECTIONS PAGE —
SO YOU CAN RETURN TO THEM WHENEVER YOU WANT TO
MAKE YOUR PARTNER FEEL SEEN, LOVED, OR ENCOURAGED.
AND THEN, USE THEM OFTEN. WORDS ARE FREE, THEIR IMPACT IS PRICELESS.

REFLECTIONS

....

....

....

....

....

....

....

....

....

....

....

....

....

DATE ACCOMPLISHED: .... ♡

Looking Back on This Season Together

This week, you get your first opportunity to pause and reflect on your journey.

It's easy to move from one week to the next without noticing all the little moments that matter—the stories shared, the laughter, the challenges, the growth.

That's why this week is about slowing down, appreciating what you've created together, and holding onto the big and small memories that shaped this season.

There's no such thing as a perfect three months . Maybe it was busy. Perhaps it felt overwhelming. Often life doesn't go exactly as planned. But you're still here. Still learning. Still growing. And that is always worth celebrating.

Try This:

Take a moment together and ask each other:

- What's one moment from the past few months I'll never forget?

- What did I learn about you — or about us — that surprised me?

- What challenge did we handle well — maybe even better than expected?

- Where do I see that we've grown as a couple?

- What am I looking forward to in the next few weeks or months?

WRITE YOUR ANSWERS ON THE REFLECTIONS PAGE –
AS A REMINDER OF HOW FAR YOU'VE ALREADY COME IN JUST A FEW WEEKS!

REFLECTIONS

....

....

....

....

....

....

....

....

....

....

....

....

....

....

DATE ACCOMPLISHED: .... ♡

WHAT HELPS YOU FEEL CALM, GROUNDED, OR PEACE-FUL, ESPECIALLY WHEN LIFE GETS BUSY?

Reflection:

We all have different ways of recharging our energy.

For some, it's quiet time alone with a book or music.

For others, it's movement, fresh air, or a cozy moment together.

This question isn't just about self-care—it's about understanding how to better support each other when life feels overwhelming.

Try This:

Each of you shares:

- What helps me reset when I'm stressed?

- What's something my partner could offer me in those moments?

> WRITE DOWN YOUR IDEAS ON THE REFLECTIONS PAGE —
> SO YOU HAVE A CALM PLAN READY FOR FUTURE BUSY DAYS.

Examples could be:

- *"Let's go for a walk together."*

- *"Give me space for 30 minutes without interruption."*

- *"Remind me to slow down and breathe."*

REFLECTIONS

....

....

....

....

....

....

....

....

....

....

....

....

....

DATE ACCOMPLISHED: .... ♡

WHAT'S ONE THING YOU'RE PROUD OF?

Reflection:

We often focus so much on ourselves as a couple, but this week is about turning the spotlight on *you* as an individual.

It's important to make space to celebrate the things you've worked hard for, the qualities you've grown into, and the goals you've quietly achieved — even if no one else noticed.

Confidence deepens when we speak our strengths out loud. And it means even more when someone we love gets to witness that.

This is your moment to be seen — and to be celebrated.

Try This:

Take turns answering:

- What's something I'm genuinely proud of — about myself or something I've done?
- What quality, choice, or action feels like a personal win?
- Where have I grown recently, even if it's still a work in progress?

Then, switch roles: Tell your partner what *you* admire most about them — something you see that maybe they forget to acknowledge in themselves.

WRITE THESE WORDS OF PRIDE AND CELEBRATION ON YOUR REFLECTIONS PAGE — THEY'RE REMINDERS TO COME BACK TO ON THE DAYS WHEN SELF-DOUBT CREEPS IN.

REFLECTIONS

....

....

....

....

....

....

....

....

....

....

....

....

....

DATE ACCOMPLISHED: .... ♡

WHAT HELPS YOU FEEL COMFORTED AND REASSURED, WHEN I (UNINTENTIONALLY) MESS UP OR HURT YOU?

Reflection:

Mistakes and misunderstandings are part of every relationship. What matters most is not avoiding them, but knowing how to repair and reconnect when they happen.

Everyone needs comfort in different ways: Some feel reassured by words. Some need physical closeness or a calming presence. Some need time and space before they're ready to talk.

This week is about learning what comfort and repair look like for each of you — so you can respond with care when it really counts. Knowing this now can turn future bumps into opportunities for deeper trust.

Try This:

Take turns sharing:

- What helps me feel comforted after we've had a disagreement or tough moment?

- What kind of apology feels sincere and real to me — words, actions, time, or something else?

- What do I most appreciate when we're trying to reconnect?

WRITE YOUR ANSWERS ON THE REFLECTIONS PAGE —
THESE NOTES BECOME YOUR PERSONAL REPAIR GUIDE, READY TO SUPPORT YOU THE NEXT TIME ONE OF YOU NEEDS A LITTLE EXTRA UNDERSTANDING.

REFLECTIONS

....

....

....

....

....

....

....

....

....

....

....

....

....

....

DATE ACCOMPLISHED: .... ♡

HOW DO WE HANDLE OUTSIDE INFLUENCE — FROM FAMILY, FRIENDS, OR SOCIAL EXPECTATIONS — IN OUR RELATIONSHIP?

Reflection:

Every couple exists in a broader world — one filled with opinions, advice, and expectations from people who mean well... and sometimes from those who don't.

Whether it's about how you spend time, make decisions, handle conflict, or define your roles, outside voices can have an impact, even when you don't realize it.

This week is about naming those influences, talking about how they've shaped (or challenged) your relationship, and exploring how to create a more solid sense of *us* — one that feels authentic and protected from unnecessary pressure.

Try This:

Ask each other:

- In what ways have outside opinions influenced how we think or act in our relationship?

- Are there situations where I feel more sensitive to other people's input — and why?

- What helps us stay grounded in *our* values when others have strong opinions?

The more grounded you feel in your shared decisions, the easier it becomes to hear others without losing your own center.

WRITE YOUR REFLECTIONS ON THE REFLECTIONS PAGE — AND CONSIDER NAMING ONE WAY YOU CAN BETTER SUPPORT EACH OTHER THE NEXT TIME OUTSIDE VOICES GET LOUD.

REFLECTIONS

....

....

....

....

....

....

....

....

....

....

....

....

....

....

DATE ACCOMPLISHED: .... ♡

WHAT'S A HAPPY MEMORY FROM YOUR CHILDHOOD THAT STILL MAKES YOU SMILE?

Reflection:

Our early memories shape the way we see love, safety, and connection — even if we're not always aware of it.

This week is about storytelling and discovery. It's a chance to learn more about the people and moments that made your partner who they are today.

And it's also a lovely way to share joy and nostalgia.

Try This:

Ask each other:

- What's one happy or funny memory I carry from my childhood?

- Why does it still stand out to me?

- What does this memory say about what makes me feel loved or at home?

WRITE A FAVORITE DETAIL OR INSIGHT ON THE REFLECTIONS PAGE — AND LET THIS MEMORY OPEN A WINDOW INTO YOUR PAST.

REFLECTIONS

....

....

....

....

....

....

....

....

....

....

....

....

....

DATE ACCOMPLISHED: .... ♡

WHAT WOULD IT LOOK LIKE IF YOU COULD DESIGN YOUR PERFECT DAY TOGETHER?

Reflection:

You can learn a lot about someone by asking them what their *ideal* day looks like. This question invites you to dream, reflect, and maybe even plan something simple but meaningful together. You might be surprised how little it takes to feel fulfilled and connected.

Sometimes, we think we need grand adventures to feel joy, but often, our "perfect day" is full of simple things:

- Good food.

- Relaxed time together.

- Laughter.

- Feeling at ease.

Try This:

Each of you describes:

- What would we do from morning to night on a perfect day together?

- Where would we be? What would the energy feel like?

- What does this dream day tell us about what we want more of in real life?

It's totally up to you whether you pick a weekday or a day off—if you're feeling inspired, do both!

WRITE DOWN YOUR ANSWERS ON THE REFLECTIONS PAGE —
AND CONSIDER MAKING SPACE FOR A MINI VERSION OF IT SOMETIME SOON.

REFLECTIONS

....

....

....

....

....

....

....

....

....

....

....

....

....

....

DATE ACCOMPLISHED: .... ♡

WHAT'S SOMETHING SMALL I DO THAT YOU APPRECIATE, BUT MAYBE I DON'T REALIZE?

Reflection:

Appreciation is one of the simplest ways to strengthen your connection, yet it's easy to overlook the little things that mean a lot.

When love becomes part of the everyday routine, some gestures become invisible. But naming them helps your partner feel seen and valued.

This week is about noticing the quiet acts of care that make a big difference.

Try This:

Ask each other:

- What's something you do regularly that makes my life easier or sweeter?

- Is there a kind habit or gesture I've never really thanked you for?

- What do I want to appreciate more out loud?

WRITE YOUR ANSWERS ON THE REFLECTIONS PAGE
— THESE ARE YOUR HIDDEN LOVE NOTES, WAITING TO BE ACKNOWLEDGED.

REFLECTIONS

....

....

....

....

....

....

....

....

....

....

....

....

....

....

DATE ACCOMPLISHED: .... ♡

WHAT'S THE BEST WAY FOR ME TO ASK FOR SPACE — WITHOUT HURTING YOU?

Reflection:

Needing space is human. It doesn't mean you love your partner less — it means you know how to take care of your own energy first – and, therefore, can show up more energized for each other.

The tricky part is that asking for space can feel like rejection if we don't talk about this openly.

This conversation helps you understand what space means to both of you and how to ask for it kindly.

Try This:

Each of you shares:

- How do I know when I need space?

- What is it that I need in this moment most?

- What's a loving way to ask for it?

WRITE THESE PHRASES DOWN ON YOUR REFLECTIONS PAGE — THEY ARE YOUR GENTLE BOUNDARY TOOLS.

Example phrases might be:

- *"I love you — I just need some quiet time to recharge right now"*

- *"Can I have an hour to myself so I can return feeling present?"*

- *"I really want to continue doing this with you - tomorrow, please."*

REFLECTIONS

....

....

....

....

....

....

....

....

....

....

....

....

....

....

DATE ACCOMPLISHED: .... ♡

WHAT'S ONE SMALL WAY TO ADD MORE LOVE INTO OUR ORDINARY ROUTINES?

Reflection:

Big romantic gestures are lovely — but often, it's the quiet, everyday moments that shape how loved we feel: In the kitchen. In the car. On the way to work. At the end of a long day.

This week is about weaving little moments of love into the flow of your daily life — so that connection becomes part of the rhythm, not just a special occasion.

Even the simplest act can say, *"I see you. I care."*

Try This:

Take turns sharing:

- What's something small that would help me feel more connected during an ordinary day?

- What loving habit would make our routine feel a little warmer?

- Where could we naturally add a moment of care, without adding more to our to-do list?

WRITE YOUR IDEAS ON THE REFLECTIONS PAGE, AND PICK ONE TO TRY THIS WEEK. YOU MIGHT BE SURPRISED HOW MUCH A SMALL HABIT CAN SHIFT THE FEELING OF YOUR EVERYDAY LIFE TOGETHER.

Examples Might Include:

- *A good morning or goodnight kiss, no matter how the day went.*

- *Leaving a kind note for your partner to find.*

- *A short "How was your day?" check-in during dinner or bedtime.*

REFLECTIONS

....

....

....

....

....

....

....

....

....

....

....

....

....

....

DATE ACCOMPLISHED: .... ♡

WHAT'S SOMETHING YOU'RE LOOKING FORWARD TO IN THE NEXT YEAR — BIG OR SMALL — THAT INVOLVES BOTH OF US?

Reflection:

It's easy to fall into the rhythm of daily routines, but looking ahead with intention can breathe new life into your relationship.

This isn't just about big trips or life-changing events (though those can be wonderful). Often, it's the small things that feel just as meaningful: a weekend away, a dinner with friends, a family tradition, or simply an afternoon with no distractions and time to reconnect.

Having something to look forward to — together — helps you stay connected and focused on what you're building.

Try This:

Ask each other:

- What am I really looking forward to sharing with you this coming week/ month/ year?

- What kind of moments or experiences would help us grow closer?

- What would I love to make space for in the coming months?

A shared plan, no matter how small, is a little promise to keep growing forward together

WRITE YOUR ANSWERS ON THE REFLECTIONS PAGE — AND CHOOSE ONE TO START PLANNING, EVEN IF IT'S SOMETHING SIMPLE.

REFLECTIONS

....

....

....

....

....

....

....

....

....

....

....

....

....

....

DATE ACCOMPLISHED: .... ♡

WHAT DO YOU THINK IS ONE OF MY GREATEST STRENGTHS — AND WHAT'S ONE AREA WHERE I COULD GROW?

Reflection:

Loving someone well means seeing both who they are *now* and who they are becoming.

This isn't about pointing out flaws — it's about noticing what's already beautiful, and gently naming the potential you see in each other.

Done with care, this kind of honesty builds trust, encouragement, and emotional safety. It's a way of saying, *"I see you. I believe in you."*

Try This:

Ask each other:

- What's something I admire about who you are, or how you show up in our relationship?

- Where do I already see growth in you?

- What's one area where I believe you could step into something even more fully?

Let this be a conversation rooted in care and encouragement.

> WRITE YOUR REFLECTIONS ON THE REFLECTIONS PAGE —
> AND SPEAK YOUR ANSWERS WITH KINDNESS.
> THIS IS A MOMENT TO LIFT EACH OTHER UP, NOT TO CRITIQUE.

REFLECTIONS

....

....

....

....

....

....

....

....

....

....

....

....

....

DATE ACCOMPLISHED: .... ♡

WHAT'S SOMETHING PLAYFUL OR SILLY WE USED TO DO THAT WE COULD BRING BACK INTO OUR RELATIONSHIP?

Reflection:

Playfulness adds energy and joy to a relationship, especially when life feels busy or serious.

Laughter creates connection. Shared silliness builds trust. And sometimes, returning to the things that made you laugh or light up together is all it takes to feel close again.

This week is about making space for the lighter side of love — and remembering how good it feels to be playful *together.*

Try This:

Take turns sharing:

- What's something playful, silly, or fun we used to do together?

- What makes me laugh or feel lighthearted when we're just being "us"?

- What's something small we could do this week just for fun — with no goal other than to enjoy each other?

WRITE YOUR IDEAS ON THE REFLECTIONS PAGE —
AND TRY ONE THIS WEEK. LAUGHTER IS A BEAUTIFUL PART OF LOVE.

Ideas Might Include:

- *Bringing back an inside joke or a made-up nickname*

- *Rewatching a funny show or video you both love*

- *Having a dance party in the kitchen or playing a goofy game*

- *Planning a date with zero "to-dos" — just joy*

REFLECTIONS

....

....

....

....

....

....

....

....

....

....

....

....

....

....

DATE ACCOMPLISHED: .... ♡

CELEBRATING A MILESTONE:

YOU'RE HALFWAY THROUGH YOUR
ONE YEAR FOR LOVE JOURNEY

You've made it to week 26 of your One Year of questions — and that's something to celebrate! Take a moment to enjoy the feeling of progress and reflect on what you've learned along the way.

✧

This week is about acknowledging your shared wins, noticing what's shifted, and thinking ahead to the second half of your journey.

Hopefully, these past months were filled with meaningful moments — some joyful, some challenging, some quiet and reflective, others full of laughter or surprise.

Maybe life got busy, and you missed a week (or a few). That's okay. What matters is that you're still here—still showing up, still choosing growth, in your own time and your own way.

Use this opportunity to explore together:

- What moments from the past few months do I want to remember?

- What was harder than expected — and how did we get through it together?

- Where did we surprise ourselves — or each other?

- What am I especially proud of in how we've navigated life as a couple?

- What do I want to bring more of into the next 12 weeks?

WRITE YOUR THOUGHTS ON THE REFLECTIONS PAGE — OR SIMPLY TALK THEM THROUGH.
THIS IS YOUR SPACE TO HONOR HOW FAR YOU'VE COME —
AND LOOK AHEAD WITH CURIOSITY, CLARITY, AND CARE.

REFLECTIONS

....

....

....

....

....

....

....

....

....

....

....

....

....

DATE ACCOMPLISHED: .... ♡

WHAT HELPS YOU FEEL MOST CONNECTED TO ME WHEN LIFE GETS HECTIC?

Reflection:

Every couple goes through seasons when life feels full, maybe even a little over-whelming.

During those times, staying connected isn't about adding more to your plate. It's about finding small moments of closeness that fit into your real life.

This week, discuss how you can feel cared for and connected, even when your time and energy are limited.

Try This:

Take a moment to share:

- What makes me feel close to you when we're both busy or tired?
- What's something small you already do that helps me feel seen?
- What could we try in the next busy week to stay connected?

WRITE YOUR ANSWERS ON THE REFLECTIONS PAGE, AND PICK ONE NEW HABIT OR RITUAL TO TRY OUT.

REFLECTIONS

....

....

....

....

....

....

....

....

....

....

....

....

....

DATE ACCOMPLISHED: .... ♡

WHAT'S ONE THING ABOUT OUR RELATIONSHIP THAT YOU'RE GENUINELY PROUD OF?

Reflection:

It's easy to focus on what needs fixing or improving, but celebrating what's already good is just as important.

This week you pause to take a closer look at who you are at this moment. It's about naming the strengths you've built together, the challenges you've overcome, and the small things that make your relationship special.

Try This:

Ask each other:

- What do I admire about us as a couple?

- What do we handle well together, even if nobody else sees it?

- What's a moment from the past months that reminded me how lucky I am to have you?

WRITE YOUR ANSWERS ON THE REFLECTIONS PAGE —
THEY'RE THE FOUNDATION OF WHAT MAKES YOUR RELATIONSHIP STRONG.

Reflections

....

....

....

....

....

....

....

....

....

....

....

....

....

Date accomplished: .... ♡

HOW CAN I BEST SHOW UP WHEN YOU FEEL VULNERABLE OR INSECURE?

Reflection:

Being in a relationship means being there for each other, not just in easy moments but also in sensitive ones.

This question is about learning how to create safety, comfort, and presence when your partner needs it most.

It's not about saying the perfect thing but knowing what helps.

Try This:

Ask each other:

- When I'm feeling low or unsure, what helps me feel safe and supported?

- Is there something I'd love to hear or feel in those moments?

- What's one thing I should avoid doing because it makes me feel worse?

WRITE DOWN YOUR ANSWERS ON THE REFLECTIONS PAGE.
IT WILL BE YOUR GUIDE TO BEING A SAFE PLACE FOR EACH OTHER.

REFLECTIONS

....

....

....

....

....

....

....

....

....

....

....

....

....

....

DATE ACCOMPLISHED: .... ♡

WHAT'S IMPORTANT TO YOU WHEN WE MAKE DECISIONS AS A COUPLE?

Reflection:

Every couple has their own way of making decisions — and it's not always something we talk about openly.

Some people like to think things through on their own first, while others prefer to talk it out from the start. Sometimes, one of you might take the lead, while the other prefers to go with the flow — until something feels off.

This week is about bringing awareness to how you each approach decisions — so you can move forward more intentionally, and with more understanding.

It's not about doing everything the same way. It's about learning how to collaborate in a way that feels fair, respectful, and balanced for both of you.

Try This:

Ask each other:

- What helps me feel included and heard when we're making decisions together?

- Do I tend to lead, follow, avoid, or overthink — and how does that impact us?

- What kind of decisions do I want us to always make together?

Even a small shift in how you approach decisions can create more trust, clarity, and ease in your relationship.

WRITE YOUR THOUGHTS ON THE REFLECTIONS PAGE —
AND NOTE ANYTHING YOU'D LIKE TO DO DIFFERENTLY MOVING FORWARD.

REFLECTIONS

....

....

....

....

....

....

....

....

....

....

....

....

....

....

DATE ACCOMPLISHED: .... ♡

WHAT'S ONE OF YOUR FAVORITE MEMORIES OF US — AND WHY DOES IT STAND OUT TO YOU?

Reflection:

Our memories tell the story of who we are as a couple.

Some moments stay with us not because they were perfect, but because of how they made us feel. They remind us of laughter, connection, or simply being completely ourselves together.

This week is about looking back with gratitude for the moments that shaped your journey so far.

Try This:

Ask each other:

- What's a moment from our relationship that I think about with a smile?

- Why does that memory matter to me?

- What does it say about what I value in us?

WRITE YOUR MEMORIES ON THE REFLECTIONS PAGE
AND DISCUSS HOW YOU MIGHT CREATE MORE MOMENTS LIKE THESE.

REFLECTIONS

....

....

....

....

....

....

....

....

....

....

....

....

....

....

....

DATE ACCOMPLISHED: .... ♡

HOW CAN WE HANDLE DISAGREEMENTS IN A LOVING AND RESPECTFUL WAY?

Reflection:

Disagreements are part of every relationship — it's how you move through them that matters most.

Some conflict brings things to the surface that need attention. But it's easy to forget that you're still on the same team even during a disagreement.

This week is about creating space for both perspectives — and finding ways to stay kind and connected, even when emotions run high.

Learning to navigate challenging moments with care can deepen your trust and strengthen your partnership.

Try This:

Take turns sharing:

- What helps me stay calm and open during a disagreement?

- What usually makes it harder for me to listen or respond kindly?

- What can we both practice to make these moments feel safer and more respectful?

Even a few small agreements can make all the difference.

WRITE A FEW IDEAS ON YOUR REFLECTIONS PAGE—
SIMPLE GROUND RULES YOU CAN REFER TO NEXT TIME THINGS FEEL TENSE.

REFLECTIONS

....

....

....

....

....

....

....

....

....

....

....

....

....

DATE ACCOMPLISHED: .... ♡

WHAT'S ONE LITTLE THING I COULD DO MORE OFTEN THAT WOULD BRIGHTEN YOUR DAY?

Reflection:

Big gestures can be beautiful, but it's the small, consistent acts of care that make love feel safe and real on a daily basis.

This week, take the opportunity to learn more about what lights up your partner's day in an ordinary moment. It might be a word, a look, a shared routine, or a tiny surprise.

Those little things are often the first to slip away when life gets busy—and the first to bring joy when we return to them.

Try This:

Ask each other:

- What small gesture makes me feel cared for?

- Is there something you've done before that I'd love to see more often?

- What's a new little habit or surprise I'd appreciate?

WRITE YOUR findINGS ON THE REFLECTIONS PAGE AND USE THEM THROUGHOUT THE COMING WEEK TO CAST A SMILE ON YOUR PARTNER'S FACE.

REFLECTIONS

....

....

....

....

....

....

....

....

....

....

....

....

....

....

DATE ACCOMPLISHED: .... ♡

WHAT FEELS TRUE TO WHO I AM — THAT I'D LOVE FOR YOU TO REALLY SEE AND UNDERSTAND?

Reflection:

There are parts of us that don't always make it into everyday conversation.

Not because we're hiding — but because they're subtle, layered, or just haven't been asked about.

This week is about shining a gentle light on your inner truths—the values, quirks, thoughts, or stories that help shape who you are.

It's a chance to say: "This is me — and it matters to me that you see this."

And for your partner to say: "I see it — and I'm listening."

Try This:

Ask each other:

- What's something deeply personal to me that I don't often share, but that is important for you to understand?

- When do I feel most like myself in our relationship?

- Was there a key moment in my life that stayed with me — one that reflects something true about who I am?

When you feel seen as yourself, love becomes even more honest and real.

WRITE YOUR REFLECTIONS ON THE REFLECTIONS PAGE — NOT JUST TO BE SEEN, BUT TO FEEL SAFE IN YOUR OWN SKIN WITHIN THE RELATIONSHIP.

REFLECTIONS

....

....

....

....

....

....

....

....

....

....

....

....

....

....

DATE ACCOMPLISHED: .... ♡

WHAT'S ONE THING YOU'RE GRATEFUL FOR ABOUT ME OR OUR RELATIONSHIP?

Reflection:

Gratitude helps us shift our focus — from what's missing or stressful to what's already good.

In the middle of daily routines, it's easy to overlook the small gestures, shared strengths, or quiet consistencies that keep your relationship strong.

This week is about taking a moment to name what you appreciate — in each other, and in the life you're building together.

It's a simple way to reconnect with the heart of your partnership.

Try This:

Take turns sharing:

- What's something I've felt especially grateful for recently — about you or about us?

- Is there something you consistently do that I may not thank you for enough?

- What part of our relationship makes me feel supported or at peace?

A little gratitude goes a long way — especially when it's spoken out loud, or written down.

WRITE YOUR ANSWERS ON THE REFLECTIONS PAGE. THESE WORDS CAN BE POWERFUL REMINDERS FOR TIMES WHEN LIFE FEELS A LITTLE OFF TRACK.

REFLECTIONS

....

....

....

....

....

....

....

....

....

....

....

....

....

DATE ACCOMPLISHED: .... ♡

WHAT VALUES OR PRINCIPLES MATTER MOST TO YOU IN OUR RELATIONSHIP?

Reflection:

Shared values act like a compass in your relationship, helping you navigate life more smoothly, especially when things feel unclear or overwhelming. It's not about being the same in every way, but about naming the guiding principles that support how you love, listen, and handle challenges together.

Some values will feel big and universal, others more personal and specific to your relationship. What matters is discovering what's truly important to each of you — and making space to honor it.

Try This:

Start by reading through this list of example values. Notice which words feel true for you — and for your relationship. You can choose a few or add your own.

Ask each other: Which values feel most important to me in love and partnership?

WRITE YOUR SHARED VALUES ON THE REFLECTIONS PAGE — THEY CAN BECOME YOUR LITTLE COMPASS FOR THE FUTURE.

Example Relationship Values:

Trust	Support	Gratitude
Honesty	Teamwork	Stability
Kindness	Curiosity	Independence
Patience	Growth	Quality Time
Loyalty	Calm	Empathy
Playfulness	Safety	Compassion
Adventure	Vulnerability	Communication
Openness	Humor	Love Without Conditions
Respect	Forgiveness	Freedom To Be Ourselves
Appreciation	Simplicity	Presence (Being Fully There)

REFLECTIONS

....

....

....

....

....

....

....

....

....

....

....

....

....

DATE ACCOMPLISHED: .... ♡

WHAT'S SOMETHING NEW YOU'D LOVE US TO LEARN OR TRY TOGETHER?

Reflection:

Trying new things together keeps your relationship curious, playful, and alive. Shared learning creates fresh energy — and gives you new stories to tell.

It's not about mastering a skill or being good at something immediately. It's about showing up openly, being adventurous, and creating memories outside your usual routines.

Try This:

Take turns asking each other:

- What's something I've always wanted to try for fun?

- Is there a skill or hobby we could learn together, even if it's small?

- What kind of experience would help us feel connected in a new way?

WRITE DOWN YOUR IDEAS ON THE REFLECTIONS PAGE — THEN CHOOSE ONE TO EXPLORE TOGETHER IN THE NEXT FEW MONTHS.

This could be anything:

- *Cooking a new dish.*

- *Learning a few words in another language.*

- *Watching DIY videos online and starting a creative project together.*

- *Or simply saying yes to something outside your comfort zone.*

REFLECTIONS

....

....

....

....

....

....

....

....

....

....

....

....

....

....

DATE ACCOMPLISHED: .... ♡

HOW DO YOU HANDLE CHANGE, AND WHAT HELPS YOU FEEL GROUNDED WHEN THINGS SHIFT?

Reflection:

Change is a natural part of life, and everyone responds differently. Some people love change and see it as exciting; others need time, routine, and reassurance to adjust.

Understanding your partner's way of navigating change helps prevent misunderstandings. This conversation will prepare you to support each other through life's transitions with patience and care.

Try This:

Ask each other:

- Do I tend to embrace change, or resist it?
- What is a good example for this from the recent past?
- What helps me feel calm when life feels uncertain?
- How can we support each other when things shift?

WRITE DOWN YOUR ANSWERS ON THE REFLECTIONS PAGE, AND TALK ABOUT HOW YOU'VE HANDLED CHANGES WELL IN THE PAST.

REFLECTIONS

....

....

....

....

....

....

....

....

....

....

....

....

....

....

DATE ACCOMPLISHED: .... ♡

STRONG, STEADY AND STILL CURIOUS!

You've made it to the next milestone together: Your third quarterly reflection. Something both of you can be really proud of!

This week is another opportunity to pause, reflect, and celebrate your progress.

How did the experience differ from the previous check-in? Do you feel like you're getting into a rhythm, or did new challenges present themselves?

Use this week to reflect on what worked well and what needs improvement during the last chapters of this journey.

Use this page to ask each other:

- What did these past 12 weeks teach me about myself and us as a couple?

- What felt especially good, fun, or nourishing for our relationship?

- What was harder than expected — and how did we navigate it together?

- What is one small moment I'll remember from these past months?

- What would I like to do more of (or less of) in the months ahead?

- What's one thing I feel grateful for right now in our relationship?

WRITE YOUR ANSWERS ON THE REFLECTIONS PAGE, AND LET THEM BE YOUR REMINDER THAT LOVE GROWS IN SMALL, ORDINARY MOMENTS – AND WHEN YOU TAKE THE TIME TO NOTICE IT.

REFLECTIONS

....

....

....

....

....

....

....

....

....

....

....

....

....

....

DATE ACCOMPLISHED: .... ♡

WHAT'S SOMETHING THAT'S JUST MINE — THAT I'D LIKE TO SHARE WITH YOU, OR PROTECT FOR MYSELF?

Reflection:

Even in the closest relationships, we all need space to be fully ourselves.

Personal hobbies, interests, and passions help us feel grounded, inspired, and whole. If yours align perfectly with your partner's — same job, same friends, same hobbies — that's wonderfully rare (and very movie-worthy). But in real life, most couples don't overlap one hundred percent. You might even lean toward the other end of the spectrum — maybe work keeps you apart most of the month, or you each have your own circles of friends, interests, and routines, only sharing meals at home.

And then, of course, there's everything in between. Every couple has its own dynamic. What matters most is understanding what works for **you.**

This week is about getting curious: Where do you each fall on that spectrum? What does balance look like in your relationship, and how can your individual needs coexist in a way that feels supportive for both of you?

Try this:

Ask each other:

- Where do we fall on the spectrum of togetherness vs. independence?

- What's something I do just for me - and would I like to share it, or keep it personal?

- How can we support each other in honoring our differences while staying connected?

WRITE YOUR ANSWERS ON THE REFLECTIONS PAGE, AND DISCUSS HOW YOUR NEEDS CAN OVERLAP OR COMPLEMENT ONE ANOTHER WITHOUT CONFLICT.

If you're struggling with this question, revisit Week 5 (Boundaries = Care). Protecting your own space doesn't mean rejecting your partner — it means honoring your needs so you can show up as your best self in the relationship.

REFLECTIONS

....

....

....

....

....

....

....

....

....

....

....

....

....

....

DATE ACCOMPLISHED: .... ♡

WHAT'S A "WILD DREAM" YOU HAVE FOR YOUR LIFE, EVEN IF IT FEELS FAR AWAY?

Reflection:

Planning gives your relationship a sense of direction—even if you never follow the exact map. Dreaming up future adventures or goals together is a fun and inspiring activity. It helps you understand what lights your partner up, what gives their life meaning, and where their heart quietly wants to go.

This week is about daring to dream big — not because you need to make it all happen immediately, but because sharing your vision is an intimate and vulnerable act. When you share your dream with someone, you're saying, "This is part of who I am."

Even if your dream feels far away or "impractical", speaking it out loud is a powerful way to be known — and to feel supported. Some dreams are meant to come true. Others simply bring you closer just by being shared.

Try This:

Ask each other:

- What's something I've always dreamed of doing, even if it feels far away?

- Why does this dream matter to me?

- How can we support each other's long-term hopes?

> WRITE YOUR ANSWERS ON THE REFLECTIONS PAGE —
> THEY'RE SEEDS YOU MIGHT WATER ONE DAY, TOGETHER.

REFLECTIONS

....

....

....

....

....

....

....

....

....

....

....

....

....

....

DATE ACCOMPLISHED: .... ♡

WHAT'S SOMETHING ABOUT YOU THAT INSPIRES ME — AND HOW DOES THAT SHAPE WHO I WANT TO BE?

Reflection:

Inspiration often starts quietly — in the way someone speaks, carries themselves, handles stress, or shows up for others. Sometimes we're aware of it in the moment. Other times, we realize it only in hindsight.

This week is about slowing down to notice: *What about you truly inspires me?*

It could be your partner's patience, determination, sense of humor, generosity, or something else entirely. Whatever it is, naming it out loud not only expresses your admiration, but also strengthens your connection.

Try This:

Ask each other:

- What do I admire most about how you live, work, love, or lead?
- Is there a moment I've seen you do something that made me want to rise a little higher, or soften a little more?
- How has being with you shaped the person I am today?

When love includes admiration, it becomes a source of inspiration!

WRITE YOUR ANSWERS ON THE REFLECTIONS PAGE —
NOT JUST TO APPRECIATE YOUR PARTNER, BUT TO REFLECT ON THE BEAUTIFUL WAYS
YOU'VE GROWN THROUGH THIS RELATIONSHIP.

REFLECTIONS

. . . .

. . . .

. . . .

. . . .

. . . .

. . . .

. . . .

. . . .

. . . .

. . . .

. . . .

. . . .

. . . .

DATE ACCOMPLISHED: .... ♡

IS THERE SOMETHING SMALL OR SILLY THAT YOU SOMETIMES WORRY ABOUT AND I MIGHT NOT KNOW?

Reflection:

We all have little worries, and sometimes, we keep them quiet because they feel too small to mention or a bit too vulnerable to say out loud. But even small, "silly" worries can build up over time if they're not understood or acknowledged.

This week is about creating space for gentle honesty. Sometimes simply hearing, *"That makes sense,"* is all it takes to ease what's been quietly weighing on you.

Try This:

Each of you shares:

- What's something I worry about, even if I know it's not logical or likely?

- What makes me feel safe when I share a worry?

- How can we better support each other in those quiet moments of doubt?

WRITE DOWN ANYTHING YOU WANT TO REMEMBER ON THE REFLECTIONS PAGE – SOMETIMES IT IS EVEN ENOUGH TO HAVE TALKED ABOUT IT. IN THIS CASE, JUST DRAW A HEART OR SMILEY AND MARK THIS WEEK AS COMPLETED :)

REFLECTIONS

....

....

....

....

....

....

....

....

....

....

....

....

....

DATE ACCOMPLISHED: .... ♡

HOW DO WE EACH HANDLE EXPECTATIONS IN OUR RELATIONSHIP?

Reflection:

Not all expectations are communicated, but they still shape how we think, feel, and interact. We often assume our partner knows what we need, only to feel disappointed when they don't respond the way we hoped. And yet, those needs may have never been clearly shared.

Unspoken expectations are a common source of misunderstanding. Talking about them openly — with kindness and curiosity — helps prevent frustration and builds a stronger foundation of trust.

This week is your opportunity to check in: What do you expect from each other, and have those expectations been clearly communicated?

Try This:

Ask each other:

- What have I expected from you that I may not have said out loud?

- How can I express my needs more clearly, without pressure or blame?

- What expectations feel helpful — and which ones might need to shift?

Clear expectations lead to deeper connection — and fewer avoidable conflicts.

WRITE YOUR findings ON THE REflECTIONS PAGE.
THEY'LL SERVE AS A HELPFUL REMINDER OF WHAT REALLY MATTERS,
ESPECIALLY IN BUSY OR EMOTIONALLY CHARGED MOMENTS.

REFLECTIONS

....

....

....

....

....

....

....

....

....

....

....

....

....

DATE ACCOMPLISHED: .... ♡

IF WE WERE TO REINTRODUCE OURSELVES AS A COUPLE, WHAT WOULD WE SAY?

Reflection:

Over time, relationships evolve — and so do the people within them. But we don't often pause to take stock of who we are *now*, as a couple, after everything we've been through.

This week is about imagining yourselves from the outside — not as the couple you once were, or the one others think you are, but as the couple you are *becoming.*

Who are you together now? What do you value? What do you stand for? What makes you *you*?

This reflection is both playful and profound — a moment to rewrite your "about us" with fresh eyes.

Try This:

Ask each other:

- If we were to write a new introduction to our relationship, what would we include?

- How would we describe our values, our story, our strengths — right now?

- What parts of us feel most important to carry forward — and what could we let go of?

You've changed and grown. This is a chance to name who you've become together.

WRITE YOUR ANSWERS ON THE REFLECTIONS PAGE —
LIKE A NEW CHAPTER HEADING FOR THE REST OF YOUR JOURNEY.

REFLECTIONS

....

....

....

....

....

....

....

....

....

....

....

....

....

....

DATE ACCOMPLISHED: .... ♡

WHAT COULD WE SIMPLIFY OR STOP DOING THAT WOULD MAKE LIFE EASIER FOR BOTH OF US?

Reflection:

Sometimes love shows up not in doing more, but in doing *less*. Life can get complicated fast. Routines and responsibilities pile up. And before you know it, even the things that once felt good start to feel like pressure.

This week is about asking a different kind of question: *What if we let it be easier?*

Whether it's a task, a habit, or an expectation, letting go of what no longer serves you can open up space for more connection, calm, and joy.

Try This:

Ask each other:

- What's something in our routine, communication, or expectations that feels heavier than it needs to?

- Is there anything I'm doing out of obligation, not intention?

- What could we let go of, or change to bring more ease into our relationship?

Making life easier doesn't mean you care less. It means you're protecting what matters most.

WRITE YOUR THOUGHTS ON THE REFLECTIONS PAGE, AND AGREE ON ONE SMALL THING TO SIMPLIFY THIS WEEK.

Reflections

....

....

....

....

....

....

....

....

....

....

....

....

....

DATE ACCOMPLISHED: .... ♡

WHAT'S A SMALL, EVERYDAY WIN WE COULD CELEBRATE MORE OFTEN?

Reflection:

It's easy to celebrate the big things — birthdays, promotions, milestones. But the little wins? Those often go unnoticed.

Yet, those small moments—the ones where you show up, try again, finish something, or simply get through the day together—are often the ones that move your relationship forward.

This week is about noticing and appreciating those tiny victories. Because when you learn to celebrate the everyday, the ordinary starts to feel rewarding!

Try This:

Ask each other:

- What's something I did this week that might seem small, but deserves a little celebration?

- What everyday effort do I really appreciate in you, even if I don't always say it?

- How can we make space for more "mini celebrations" in our lives?

A kind word. A smile. A toast over dinner. Whatever it is, let it help you remember: *You're doing better than you think.*

WRITE YOUR ANSWERS ON THE REFLECTIONS PAGE — AND EACH CHOOSE ONE SMALL WIN TO HONOR THIS WEEK.

REFLECTIONS

....

....

....

....

....

....

....

....

....

....

....

....

....

DATE ACCOMPLISHED: .... ♡

WHAT'S SOMETHING SIMPLE THAT BRINGS YOU JOY — THAT WE COULD DO TOGETHER MORE OFTEN?

Reflection:

Joy doesn't have to be complicated — and it doesn't have to cost a thing. It often lives in the little things: a walk in nature, music in the kitchen, laughter over something silly, a shared hobby, or even just a quiet moment of rest.

This week is about noticing what lights you up and choosing to bring more of it into your everyday life. Even small moments of joy can shift the energy—within each of you and between you.

The more often you create room for these little mood-boosters, the easier they will come to you.

Try This:

Ask each other:

- What's a small activity or moment that makes me feel genuinely happy?

- Is there something we used to do that we haven't taken time for lately?

- What's one simple, joyful moment we could plan for this week?

Joy is often waiting for us. We just have to make space for it.

WRITE YOUR ANSWERS ON THE REFLECTIONS PAGE —
THEY'LL BECOME YOUR GO-TO JOY LIST WHEN LIFE FEELS DULL OR HEAVY.

Reflections

....

....

....

....

....

....

....

....

....

....

....

....

....

....

DATE ACCOMPLISHED: .... ♡

WHAT'S A COMPLIMENT OR AFFIRMATION I'VE GIVEN YOU THAT HAS STAYED WITH YOU?

Reflection:

Words have staying power. The right phrase, spoken at the right moment, can echo for years — building confidence, soothing doubt, or simply reminding you that you're loved.

This week is about noticing which words have made a lasting impact — and why. It's also a reminder that thoughtful words don't have to be grand or poetic to be meaningful. They just have to be real.

Try This:

Ask each other:

- What's something you once said that I still think about — even if you don't remember saying it?

- What kinds of compliments or encouragement feel especially meaningful to me?

- What do I wish I heard more often from you?

WRITE YOUR WORDS ON THE REFLECTIONS PAGE —
THEY'RE LITTLE REMINDERS OF HOW LANGUAGE CAN NURTURE LOVE.
THEN, SPEAK THOSE WORDS MORE OFTEN. SAY THEM OUT LOUD.
BECAUSE WHAT YOU SAY BECOMES PART OF EACH OTHER'S INNER VOICE.

REFLECTIONS

....

....

....

....

....

....

....

....

....

....

....

....

....

....

DATE ACCOMPLISHED: .... ♡

WHAT HELPS YOU TRUST ME MORE DEEPLY?

Reflection:

Trust isn't built in one moment — it's built slowly, through small, consistent actions over time. It's about knowing you can count on each other, that what's said will be followed through, and that vulnerability will be met with care.

This week is about better understanding what helps your partner feel secure and grounded in the relationship, and how you can continue to protect that trust as it grows.

Trust can be quiet — often noticed more in how someone shows up than in what they say. And when it's strong, it creates a space where love can relax, breathe, and expand.

Try This:

Ask each other:

- What actions help me feel safe, steady, and supported by you?

- How do we show up in ways that build — or rebuild — trust over time?

- Is there anything we've learned to avoid, because it erodes trust?

WRITE YOUR REFLECTIONS ON THE REFLECTIONS PAGE —
SO YOU BOTH HAVE A GUIDE TO RETURN TO WHEN TRUST NEEDS TENDING.

REFLECTIONS

....

....

....

....

....

....

....

....

....

....

....

....

....

....

DATE ACCOMPLISHED: .... ♡

WHAT'S A HOPE OR WISH FOR OUR RELATIONSHIP IN THE YEAR AHEAD?

Reflection:

As you near the end of this journey, it's the perfect moment to look forward at the endless possibilities.

This week isn't about setting goals or solving problems anymore. It's about asking: *What do I hope we grow into, together?*

Maybe you're wishing for more ease. More adventure. More gentleness. Maybe it's about rediscovering joy, discovering something new, or simply continuing what already feels good.

Try This:

Ask each other:

- What am I dreaming of for us in the next part of our relationship?

- What do I hope we'll feel more of — or less of — in the year ahead?

- What's one thing I'd love to create, experience, or protect together?

WRITE YOUR HOPES ON THE REFLECTIONS PAGE —
AS UPLIFTING INTENTIONS TO GUIDE YOU FORWARD WITH CARE AND CURIOSITY.

REFLECTIONS

....

....

....

....

....

....

....

....

....

....

....

....

....

....

DATE ACCOMPLISHED: .... ♡

Your Final Reflection - for Now

You've made it! 52 weeks of showing up for your relationship. This final week is your invitation to pause one last time: To look back with gratitude. To move ahead with curiosity.

What have you learned about each other? What surprised you? What stayed the same — and what changed? This is not the end of your journey. It's simply the end of this chapter. The habits of asking, listening, and growing together are always here for you to return to.

You might even choose to revisit this book again — weekly, monthly, or whenever you need a gentle reminder of the reflections you have shared. Let it guide you back to what lights your partner up. To what soothes you during hard days. To how you communicate, connect, and support each other with loving care.

Try This:

Ask each other:

- What am I most grateful for from this year together?
- What memory or conversation from this book will stay with me?
- How did we grow as a couple, in ways big or small?

Love isn't built in perfect weeks. It's built in presence, in effort, in coming back to each other — again and again. *This is your story. And this is only the beginning.*

WRITE YOUR ANSWERS ON THE REFLECTIONS PAGE —
TO HONOR THE STORY YOU'VE WRITTEN TOGETHER.

REFLECTIONS

....

....

....

....

....

....

....

....

....

....

....

....

....

....

DATE ACCOMPLISHED: .... ♡

Stay Connected

If you'd like more ideas, inspiration, and new books to support your communication and relationship journey, I'd love to stay connected.

You can find future releases, free resources, and more at:

www.kommor-consulting.com

You Did Something Truly Beautiful

Dear Readers,

You've asked each other meaningful questions. You've shared stories, memories, hopes, and challenges. You've created space for real connection — sometimes light and playful, sometimes honest and deep.

That's no small thing, especially in today's fast-moving world. It takes courage to slow down. It takes intention to step off autopilot and make room for real conversation. It takes dedication to keep choosing each other — again and again.

Maybe not every week went as planned. Maybe some answers felt hard to put into words. But you showed up. For yourself. For each other. For your relationship.

That's precisely what this book was about. It wasn't about having the right answers but asking the right questions. Staying curious. Truly seeing and hearing one another. And maybe even surprising each other along the way.

So, keep talking. Keep listening. Keep loving — with intention, kindness, and joy.

Your story is still being written. And I'm deeply honored that *One Year for Love* could be a small part of it.

Love grows in the space we create for it. You've just spent an entire year creating that space.

That's something worth celebrating. So go ahead — treat yourself. You've earned it.

With love and gratitude,

Alexandra

Founder of KOMMOR Consulting

PS: To keep your momentum going, take a look at the following *Bonus section*. I have prepared *three awesome tools* that you might find helpful to continue your journey!

Bonus Section:
The Couple's Connection Planner

Keep the Momentum Going

You've spent One Year asking thoughtful questions, creating space for real conversations, and deepening your connection week by week.

Now it's time to keep that energy alive — through shared experiences, rituals, and playful intentions.

This bonus section is here to help you:

- Protect time for meaningful connection with the *Plan-Your-Date* Monthly Connection Time Schedule.

- Unplug from distractions for intentional and uninterrupted time together with the

- Plan joy, presence, and shared memories into your life

You can use it monthly, seasonally, or whenever life needs a little spark. There's no "right" way — just your way.

LET IT FEEL LIGHT. LET IT FEEL EASY.
LET IT BRING YOU JOY.

BONUS 1
PLAN-YOUR-DATE
MONTHLY CONNECTION TIME SCHEDULE

Sometimes the simplest moments are the most meaningful. This bonus section is here to help you stay intentional with your time — and keep creating memorable moments together, no matter what life throws your way.

You don't need extravagant plans or fancy reservations every time. Change it up. Meaningful dates can be simple occasions where you pause, show up fully, and enjoy each other.

This planner encourages you to choose one intentional connection date per month, something you both look forward to and remember.

You can plan together, or take turns organizing a surprise day. Either way, treat it like something that matters.

Choose a specific time and place — and protect it on your calendar. Avoid last-minute cancellations, and give your shared time the same priority you'd give any important commitment.

The more clearly you define the experience, the more likely it is to happen — and to feel special.

Instead of writing "dinner out," try something like:

- "Grimaldi's Pizzeria – Try a new dish we've never ordered."
- "Sunset walk through the Botanical Garden – bring sketchbooks and wine.'
- "At-home movie night — pick a favorite childhood film and make popcorn."

The details don't need to be elaborate — they need to be intentional.

PLAN-YOUR-DATE

* JANUARY *

Where?

....

When?

....

What?

....

* FEBRUARY *

Where?

....

When?

....

What?

....

* MARCH *

Where?

....

When?

....

What?

....

* APRIL *

Where?

....

When?

....

What?

....

* MAY *

Where?

....

When?

....

What?

....

* JUNE *

Where?

....

When?

....

What?

....

Monthly Connection Time Schedule

* July *

Where?

....

When?

....

What?

....

* August *

Where?

....

When?

....

What?

....

* September *

Where?

....

When?

....

What?

....

* October *

Where?

....

When?

....

What?

....

* November *

Where?

....

When?

....

What?

....

* December *

Where?

....

When?

....

What?

....

BONUS 2
No Screen Night Tracker

Unplug to Reconnect

In a world full of distractions, one of the most powerful ways to show up for each other is to simply *be present*.

This bonus section is your invitation to unplug from screens and reconnect with what matters most: time together without notifications or background noise.

Use this space to track 12 nights where you turn off your phones and tune in to each other. Whether you go screen-free three times a week, or once a month, this tracker helps you stay intentional about it—even for just one evening at a time.

You're obviously welcome to continue the habit beyond the provided check-boxes!

Date: ....

What we did: ....

....

How was it? ....

....

Do it again? ....

Date: ....

What we did: ....

....

How was it? ....

....

Do it again? ....

Date: ....

What we did: ....

....

How was it? ....

....

Do it again? ....

Date: ....

What we did: ....

....

How was it? ....

....

Do it again? ....

Date: ....

What we did: ....

....

How was it? ....

....

Do it again? ....

Date: ....

What we did: ....

....

How was it? ....

....

Do it again? ....

Date: ....

What we did: ....

....

How was it? ....

....

Do it again? ....

Date: ....

What we did: ....

....

How was it? ....

....

Do it again? ....

Date: ....

What we did: ....

....

How was it? ....

....

Do it again? ....

Date: ....

What we did: ....

....

How was it? ....

....

Do it again? ....

Date: ....

What we did: ....

....

How was it? ....

....

Do it again? ....

Date: ....

What we did: ....

....

How was it? ....

....

Do it again? ....

BONUS 3
MINI ADVENTURE BUCKET LIST

Dream. Plan. Explore. Together.

This space is all about joyful anticipation — the places you want to go, the things you want to try, and the fun you want to create together. Not all adventures need a passport. Some just need a little imagination and a shared yes.

You might plan a weekend getaway to a romantic city for your anniversary, hike to a local lookout spot, take a beginners art class, sign up for a zipline tour, volunteer together at a community event, or finally visit that intriguing little shop you've walked past a dozen times.

Big or small, these moments bring fresh energy into your relationship — and give you something meaningful to look forward to, together.

PLACES TO VISIT (WOLDWIDE)	LOCAL HIGHLIGHTS (SPORTS, CULTURE, NATURE)

LEARN TOGETHER

ADRENALINE BOOSTERS

HELPING OTHERS

RANDOM STUFF

RESOURCES, REFERENCES & INSPIRATIONS

Brown, B. (2012). *Daring greatly: How the courage to be vulnerable transforms the way we live, love, parent, and lead*. Gotham Books.

Chapman, G. (1992). *The 5 love languages: The secret to love that lasts*. Northfield Publishing.

Gottman, J. M., & Silver, N. (2015). *The seven principles for making marriage work: A practical guide from the country's foremost relationship expert* (Revised ed.). Harmony Books.

Note to Readers:

No third-party content was quoted or reproduced. This book was written using the author's original voice and insights, with support from customer research, relationship coaching principles, and established communication practices. All external frameworks are acknowledged with gratitude and interpreted to fit the vision of One Year for Love — a gentle, open-ended guide for real connection.

www.ingramcontent.com/pod-product-compliance
Lightning Source LLC
Chambersburg PA
CBHW051632120626
46551CB00014B/2041

* 9 7 9 8 9 9 3 3 6 6 0 0 5 *